PICTURE WINDOW BOOKS
World Atlases

ATLAS of
Australia

by Karen Foster

PICTURE WINDOW BOOKS
Minneapolis, Minnesota

First American edition published in 2008 by
Picture Window Books
151 Good Counsel Drive
P.O. Box 669
Mankato, MN 56002-0669
877-845-8392
www.picturewindowbooks.com

Editors: Shelly Lyons and Jill Kalz
Designer: Hilary Wacholz
Page Production: Melissa Kes
Art Director: Nathan Gassman
Associate Managing Editor: Christianne Jones
Content Adviser: Lisa Thornquist, Ph.D., Geography
Cartographer: XNR Productions, Inc. (13, 15, 17, 19)

Editor and Compiler: Karen Foster
Factual Researcher: Joe Josephs
Designers: Fanny Masters & Maia Terry
Picture Researcher: Diana Morris
Illustrators: Rebecca Elliott and Q2 Media
Maps: Geo-Innovations UK

Printed in the United States of America.

Foster, Karen.
Atlas of Australia / by Karen Foster. – Minneapolis, MN : Picture Window Books, 2008.
32 p. : col. ill., col. maps ; cm. – (Picture Window Books world atlases).
2-4
2-4.
Includes index and glossary.
ISBN 978-1-4048-3881-9 (library binding)
ISBN 978-1-4048-3889-5 (paperback)
1. Maps–Juvenile literature. 2. Australia–Geography–Juvenile literature.
3. Australia–Maps for children.
DU105.2   919.94 REF
                                                                DLC

Photo Credits:
John Austin/Shutterstock: 22t. Howard Bernstihl Photographers Direct: 20tr. Paul Chinn/Corbis: 21b. Robert Cumming/
Shutterstock: 23cr. Jeff Curtes/Corbis: 21tr. Kurt/Dreamstime: compass rose 4, 7, 9, 11, 13, 15, 17, 19, 25, 27. Kaspars
Grinvalds/Shutterstock: 26. Damian Herde/Shutterstock: 23t. Graeme Knox/Shutterstock: 10b. Somin Krzic/Shutterstock:
23b. Frans Lanting/Corbis: 20bl. Douglas Litchfield/Shutterstock: 23cl. Robin MacKenzie/Corbis: 8. Matthew McKee/Eye
Ubiquitous/Corbis: 20br. James Osmond/Photographers Direct: 12. Carl & Ann Purcell/Corbis: 24tr. Nicholas Rjabow/
Shutterstock: 18tr. Anders Ryman/Corbis: 6. Dennis Sabo/Shutterstock: 25. Sander van Sinttrnye/Shutterstock: 9. Ian
Scott/Shutterstock: 22b. Paul A. Souders/Corbis: 24bl. Penny Tweedie/Corbis: 18bl. Patrick Ward/Corbis: 21tl. Michael S.
Yamashita/Corbis: 24br.

Editor's Note: The maps in this book were created with the Miller projection.

Table of Contents

Welcome to Australia

The world is made up of five oceans and seven chunks of land called continents: North America, South America, Antarctica, Europe, Africa, Asia, and Australia. This map shows Australia's position in the world.

Arctic Circle

NORTH AMERICA

Atlantic Ocean

Tropic of Cancer

Pacific Ocean

Equator

SOUTH AMERICA

Tropic of Capricorn

Legend
A legend tells you the title of a map and what the map's symbols mean.

SOUTH AMERICA — Continent

Pacific Ocean — Ocean

Antarctic Circle

The Antarctic Circle is an imaginary line in the southern part of the world that marks the edge of the Antarctic region.

Compass Rose
A compass rose shows you the four cardinal directions: north (N), south (S), east (E), and west (W).

4

Australia is the smallest of the continents and lies entirely beneath the equator. It is the only continent that is also a country. Australia is part of a region called Oceania, which is made up of more than 25,000 islands in the Pacific Ocean.

North Pole

Arctic Ocean

The Arctic Circle is an imaginary line in the northern part of the world that marks the edge of the Arctic region.

Arctic Circle

EUROPE

ASIA

The Tropic of Cancer and the Tropic of Capricorn are imaginary lines north and south of the equator. Places that lie between the two lines are hot and wet.

Tropic of Cancer

Pacific Ocean

AFRICA

Indian Ocean

Equator

The equator is an imaginary line around the middle of the world.

AUSTRALIA

Tropic of Capricorn

Southern Ocean

Antarctic Circle

ANTARCTICA

South Pole

Scale Bar

A scale bar helps measure distance. It tells you the difference between distances on a map and the actual distances on Earth's surface.

Miles
0   0.5   1   1.5   2   2.5

0   1   2   3   4
Kilometers

5

Countries

The continent of Australia is made up of one country–Australia. It is the sixth-largest country in the world. Because of its location beneath the equator, Australia is called the Land Down Under.

There are many islands, including New Zealand, that make up the region of Oceania. New Zealand is one of the largest countries in Oceania. It is divided into two islands–the North Island and the South Island.

A Maori child in New Zealand uses a conch shell as an instrument.

What's on the Australian menu?

barbecued fish and chicken

biscuits made of oats, coconut, and honey

cakes dipped in chocolate and coconut

lime juice cordial

macadamia nut brittle

meat pie and tomato sauce

meringue, cream, and fruit

stuffed leg of lamb

yeast-based spread on toast

Languages of Australia

Most people in Australia speak English. But before English was spoken in Australia, the Aborigine people were speaking their own languages. The Aborigine people have been living in Australia for more than 40,000 years. Today, there are more than 200 different Aboriginal languages still in use.

Languages of New Zealand

In New Zealand, the official languages are English, Maori, and New Zealand Sign Language. The Maori language comes from the Maori people, who have lived in New Zealand for about 1,000 years. New Zealand is the only country in which the Maori language is commonly spoken.

Equator

Indian Ocean

Tropic of Capricorn

AUSTRALIA

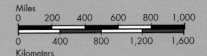

Pacific Ocean

NEW ZEALAND

N
W   E
S

AUSTRALIA

NEW ZEALAND

Landforms

Australia can be divided into three sections–the Western Plateau, the Central Lowlands, and the Eastern Highlands.

The Western Plateau covers more than 65 percent of the continent's total area. It contains a number of large deserts.

The Central Lowlands stretch across several basins.

The continent's largest mountain range is the Great Dividing Mountain Range, which is also known as the Eastern Highlands. These mountains stretch across the east coast of Australia and divide the east coast from the rest of the country.

Uluru

Also known as Ayers Rock, Uluru is a giant sandstone rock that rises out of the middle of the continent. It is 1,142 feet (348 meters) high and about 6 miles (9.6 kilometers) around its base. Uluru is one of the largest single rock formations on Earth. The native Aborigine people consider Uluru to be a holy place.

Uluru glows red during sunrises and sunsets.

The Cape York Peninsula

The Cape York Peninsula in northeastern Australia is truly wild. Almost the entire 54,000 square miles (140,400 square kilometers) of the peninsula is wilderness. There are only about 18,000 people who live on the Cape York Peninsula, and more than half of them are Aborigine people.

The Outback

The Outback makes up more than 70 percent of Australia's interior. Its landscape contains many deserts, including the Great Sandy Desert, the Gibson Desert, and the Great Victoria Desert. Deserts are not landforms, but they make up an important part of the continent's landscape. The Outback also contains the MacDonnel Mountains and Hamersley Mountains.

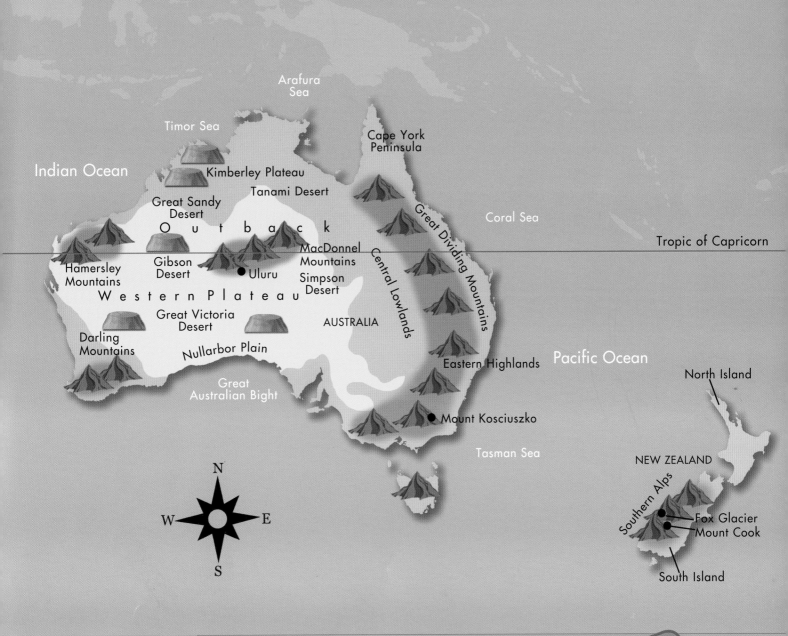

The Southern Alps stretch across the South Island of New Zealand. Mount Cook, at a height of 12,316 feet (3,756 m), is the country's highest mountain.

The Southern Alps

• The south-western part of New Zealand's North Island has several active volcanoes. In this area, there are also many hot springs.

• Fox Glacier, on New Zealand's South Island, is less than 982 feet (300 meters) above sea level.

Bodies of Water

Australia is surrounded by bodies of water. The Indian Ocean lies to the west, and the Pacific Ocean lies to the east. Many seas also border the continent. These include the Timor, the Arafura, the Coral, and the Tasman.

Some of Australia's rivers and lakes, such as Lake Eyre, are mostly dry during parts of the year. Lake Eyre is the largest lake on the continent. It is a salt lake and has completely filled with water only three times

The longest river

The Murray River is Australia's longest river. It stretches through more than 1,562 miles (2,520 kilometers) of land. During the 1800s, steamboats carried goods from one end of the river to the other. When the railroads were built, river traffic slowed. Today, people travel the Murray River mostly for fun.

The Murray River

Great Australian Bight

The Great Australian Bight is a large, open bay off the southern coast of Australia. Because it receives very little runoff from the deserts that lie to the north, the Great Australian Bight does not have much life in its waters. However, sharks and whales are known to show up there.

Lake Taupo

Lake Taupo is located on New Zealand's North Island. It is the largest freshwater lake in the country. Underneath its still, blue waters lies the world's most destructive volcano. But it hasn't erupted in the past 26,000 years. A volcano is a kind of mountain that can throw hot, melted rock (lava), ashes, and gases from deep inside the earth.

Lake Taupo

Major Bodies of Water

● place of interest

lake   river

Equator

Arafura Sea

Timor Sea

Daly River

Indian Ocean

Victoria River

Fitzroy River

Coral Sea

Tropic of Capricorn

AUSTRALIA

Lake Eyre

Cooper's Creek

Barwon River

Darling River

Lachlan River

Pacific Ocean

Great Australian Bight

Murray River

Snowy Mountains

North Island

Waikato River

Lake Taupo

Wanganui River

NEW ZEALAND

Bass Strait

Tasman Sea

Cook Strait

Lake Te Anau

Waitaki River

N
W   E
S

Clutha River

DID YOU KNOW?

Waterways flowing from the Snowy Mountains in southeastern Australia have 16 dams to hold back the snow melt. Tunnels pipe the water into large rivers, sending it to dry parts of the country.

11

Climate is the average weather a place has from season to season, year to year. Rainfall and temperature play large parts in a region's climate.

Australia lies just south of the equator, so its climate is warm.

It is also very dry. In fact, Australia is the second-driest continent on Earth.

Seasons

Because Australia and New Zealand lie beneath the equator, the seasons there are opposite of those in areas such as the United States and Europe, which lie above the equator.

Summer: December to February
Fall: March to May
Winter: June to August
Spring: September to November

Tropical North

Northern Australia is tropical, with hot temperatures and a lot of humidity. Here, there are wet and dry seasons. The hotter wet season usually lasts from December to March. The cooler dry season is usually from May to October.

During the wet season, the tropical north region has still pools of water called billabongs.

Climate basics

A region's climate depends upon three major things: how close it is to the ocean, how high up it is, and how close it is to the equator. Areas along the ocean have milder climates than areas farther inland. The higher a region is, and the farther it is from the equator, the colder its temperature.

• The northeastern coast of Australia is the wettest part of the continent.

• In Australia, snow falls high in the Australian Alps and in some of the mountains of Tasmania.

| dry | dry most or all year with hot summers and warm to cold winters | mild | wet winters or all year with warm to hot summers and cool winters |

● place of interest

| tropical | wet and dry seasons, hot all year |

Equator

Arafura Sea

Timor Sea

Indian Ocean

Tropic of Capricorn

Coral Sea

AUSTRALIA

Pacific Ocean

Great Australian Bight

Australian Alps ●

Tasman Sea

NEW ZEALAND

N
W · E
S

Tasmania

South Island

- Most of New Zealand doesn't have much of a temperature change between the summer and winter months, but its coldest month is July and the warmest time is in January or February.
- In New Zealand, snow is most commonly found in the mountains and in the south and east of the South Island.

13

Plants

Because Australia is so far from other lands, many of its plants are found nowhere else in the world. They are well-adapted to the continent's ecosystems. An ecosystem is all of the living and nonliving things in a certain area. It includes plants, animals, soil, weather … everything!

In the wet rain forests that are along Australia's northeastern coast, trees grow tall and close together. Farther inland, there is less rainfall and the trees are shorter and are spread apart amid grasses and shrubs. Tough-leaved bushes are found throughout Australia's interior.

Some Plants of Australia and New Zealand

desert	saltbush	The saltbush grows in dry areas and does well in salty soil.
	boab tree	Boab trees are found only in northwestern Australia. They have very large trunks in which they store water.
	spinifex	Spinifex is a spiky grass that covers about 20 percent of Australia. It is found in sandy soil and grows in a short dome shape.
forest	eucalyptus tree	Different kinds of eucalyptus trees, or gum trees, grow all over Australia. Their leaves produce an oil that can be toxic.
forest	golden wattle	The golden wattle is Australia's national flower. It is found mostly in southeastern Australia and has long green leaves and small yellow flowers.
	kangaroo paw	The flowering plant called kangaroo paw looks like a kangaroo's hind foot. It grows naturally only in Australia's southwestern forests.
grassland	orchid	There are hundreds of different kinds of orchids in Australia. One kind grows underground and never sees sunlight. Orchids always have a large upper petal.
mountain	kauri tree	The kauri tree is found only on New Zealand's North Island. Its bark is flaky, and its leaves are leathery. It can reach a height of 165 feet (50 meters).
rain forest	mangrove tree	The mangrove tree has long roots that hold the trunk of the tree above water. The roots develop small holes through which the tree can take in air.

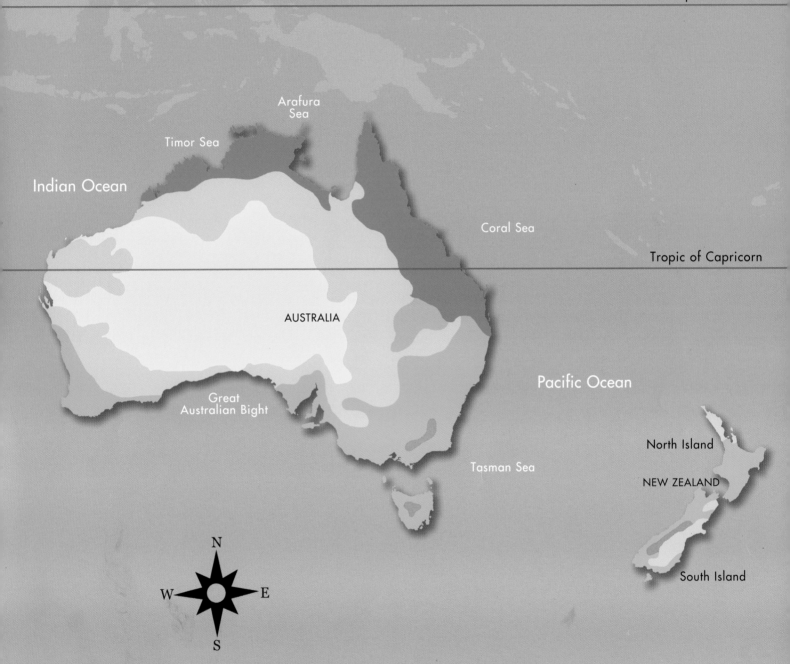

Major Ecosystems

desert	grassland	rain forest
forest	mountain	

Equator

Arafura Sea

Timor Sea

Indian Ocean

Coral Sea

Tropic of Capricorn

AUSTRALIA

Pacific Ocean

Great Australian Bight

North Island

Tasman Sea

NEW ZEALAND

South Island

N
W E
S

Animals

Because Australia is far from the other continents, many of its animals aren't found anywhere else in the world. A number of them are well-adapted to the desert ecosystem. An ecosystem is all of the living and nonliving things in a certain area.

Just off the northeastern coast of Australia lies the Great Barrier Reef. It is the world's largest coral reef. The reef is made up of skeletons that are produced by millions of small animals called coral polyps.

Some Animals of Australia and New Zealand

desert

king brown snake
The king brown snake is one of the largest snakes in Australia. It is also one of the most poisonous. It can grow to be 10 feet (3.3 meters) long.

desert death adder
The desert death adder is one of the most poisonous snakes in the world. The snake uses its tail to attract prey.

dingo
The dingo is a wild dog found in the Outback. A dingo eats kangaroos and other animals.

kangaroo
A kangaroo is a marsupial. It carries its baby in a pouch, a pocket of skin on its belly.

wombat
The wombat escapes the hot desert sun by burrowing deep underground.

forest

laughing kookaburra
The laughing kookaburra has a large head and long beak. It is famous for its call, which sounds like a human laugh.

koala
Koalas are marsupials. They feed on eucalyptus leaves and sleep about 20 hours a day.

grassland

redback spider
The redback spider is common throughout Australia. The female has a yellow or red marking on its back. Its bite is poisonous.

mountain

emu
The emu is a bird that can't fly. The emu's long, powerful legs allow it to run as fast as 30 miles (50 kilometers) per hour.

rain forest

frilled lizard
When the frilled lizard is scared, it opens its mouth and shows a collar of skin around its neck.

duck-billed platypus
The duck-billed platypus spends most of its time in ponds and streams. The platypus uses its bill to take in water and food such as shrimp, snails, and worms.

16

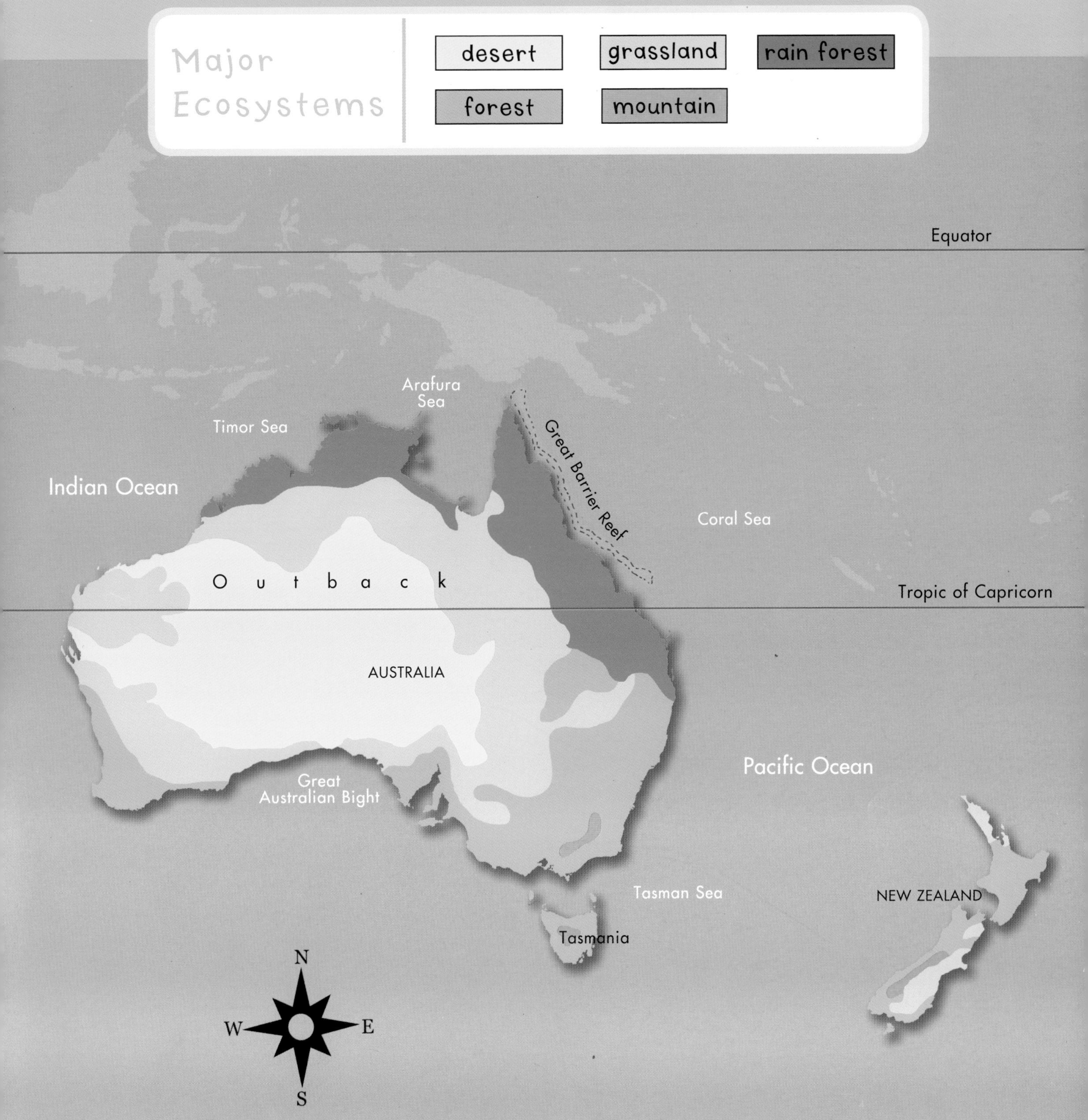

Major Ecosystems

desert   grassland   rain forest
forest   mountain

Equator

Arafura Sea

Timor Sea

Indian Ocean

Great Barrier Reef

Coral Sea

O u t b a c k

Tropic of Capricorn

AUSTRALIA

Pacific Ocean

Great Australian Bight

Tasman Sea

NEW ZEALAND

Tasmania

N
W   E
S

17

Population

Australia's population is slightly more than 20 million. Many people live in the big coastal cities, such as Sydney, Melbourne, and Brisbane because of the mild climate in those areas.

Most Australians have come from Europe. Many of them moved to Australia during the past 200 years. They enjoy the warm climate, the outdoor lifestyle, and new job opportunities. Native Aborigines make up about 1 percent of the total population.

Native people

Australia's Northern Territory is home to the largest Aboriginal population in the country. In fact, Aborigines make up about 25 percent of the Northern Territory's population. The largest Aboriginal reserve in the Northern Territory is called Arnhem Land. About 16,000 Aborigines live there.

Aborigine children

Four big cities

With about 4.1 million residents, **Sydney** is Australia's most populated city. Located on the southeastern coast, it is home to many popular beaches and famous landmarks, such as the Sydney Opera House and the Harbour Bridge.

The Sydney Opera House and Harbour Bridge

With about 3.6 million people, Australia's second-most populated city is **Melbourne**. It is home to many of Australia's largest companies, such as National Australia Bank.

Brisbane, located on the east coast of Australia, is the country's third-most populated city. It has about 1.8 million residents.

Perth is Australia's fourth-most populated city, with 1.4 million people. It is the largest city located on the west coast. Perth has the fastest-growing population of all of the major cities in Australia.

less than 5	5–25	25–125	125–250	more than 250

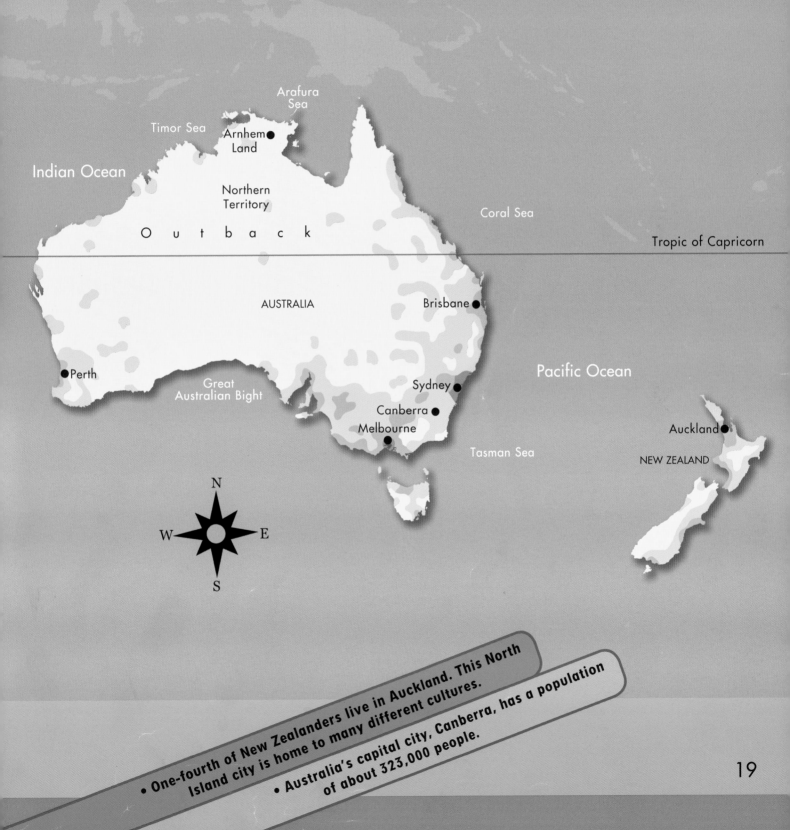

Equator

Arafura
Sea

Timor Sea

Arnhem ●
Land

Indian Ocean

Northern
Territory

O u t b a c k

Coral Sea

Tropic of Capricorn

AUSTRALIA

Brisbane ●

Perth ●

Great
Australian Bight

Pacific Ocean

Sydney ●

Canberra ●

Melbourne ●

Auckland ●

Tasman Sea

NEW ZEALAND

N
W   E
S

● One-fourth of New Zealanders live in Auckland. This North Island city is home to many different cultures.

● Australia's capital city, Canberra, has a population of about 323,000 people.

19

People and Customs

The many Australians who came from Europe carried their traditions with them. But there are people who are native to Australia as well.

The Aborigines were living in Australia long before the Europeans arrived. Their culture and traditions are very strong, and they work hard to preserve them.

Moomba Waterfest

Moomba is Australia's largest community festival. It usually takes place in March. During the festival, the Yarra River is filled with internationally known water-skiers who compete for top honors. There is also music, a parade, and a carnival.

The International Waterskiing Championships are part of Moomba Waterfest.

Aboriginal art

Aborigines paint pictures about their legends and beliefs. They paint on rocks, tree bark, the ground, and their own bodies. Many paintings show animals, patterns, or scenes from traditional stories.

Aborigines use ochre, a rock that is naturally colored with iron, to make their paints.

Aborigines paint their faces for ceremonies and other special events.

Huge distances

Families who live on sheep and cattle stations, or ranches, in the Outback often live far away from the nearest hospital. People there have developed the Royal Flying Doctor Service. These health workers use planes to fly to remote places in the Outback.

The Royal Flying Doctor Service picks up more than 90 patients a day.

Get on board

New Zealand is a popular spot for those taking skiing and snowboarding vacations. Because the ski season in New Zealand runs from July to October, people from northern parts of the world can hit the slopes here while their friends at home are feeling the summer heat.

The most popular resorts for snowboarding are Queenstown and Wanaka.

Maori dance

The Maori are the native people of New Zealand. One of their customs is to perform a dance called a *haka*. During the dance, performers stick out their tongues and show the whites of their eyes. The dance is performed for many different reasons, including celebration, welcoming guests, and preparing for war.

A haka is most often performed by men, but women may also take part in this dance.

Postcard Places

Australia is home to many natural places of interest. But it also has large cities, open spaces, and underwater wonders. All of these things combined make Australia a special continent.

Perth is in southwestern Australia. The nearest large city is more than 1,600 miles (2,560 kilometers) away.

Great Barrier Reef

Perth

Beerwah
Gold Coast

Auckland

Cathedral Cove

Great Barrier Reef

Australia's Great Barrier Reef is located just off the northeastern coast of Australia. It is so large, you can see it from space.

The Australia Zoo in Beerwah houses many endangered animals and is known for its crocodile shows.

Australia Zoo

New Zealand's Cathedral Cove is lined with parts of old volcanoes. A cove is a small, sheltered body of water along a coast.

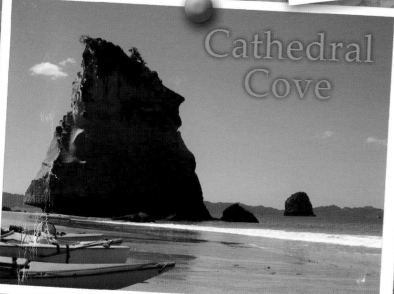

Cathedral Cove

Auckland

Auckland, located on New Zealand's North Island, is the country's largest city. It is between two harbors, Manukau and Waitemata.

Gold Coast

Australia's Gold Coast is a popular site for surfers because of its long beaches and perfect waves.

Growing and Making

Australia has a variety of major industries. It is one of the top exporters in the world of both beef and wool. The continent's farming industry also produces a lot of dairy products.

Mining is another top industry in Australia. Australians are known for producing some of the world's best opals and diamonds.

Cattle stations

Australia's cattle ranches are called stations. They are some of the largest ranches in the world. The largest cattle station in the country is Anna Creek Station in South Australia. It covers about 6 million acres (2.4 hectares). It is larger than the entire country of Belgium!

Australia's cattle stations raise cattle for beef.

Opal mining

Up to 95 percent of the world's opals come from Australia. An opal is a soft rock that shimmers and is used to make jewelry. The Coober Pedy mine is famous for its light-colored opals. The Lightning Ridge mine is famous for its black ones.

Sheep for wool

Australia produces a lot of high quality wool. Sheep farmers clip the sheep's woolly fleece as close to its skin as they can. Later, the wool is packed into bales and sent away to be sold.

A sheep farmer clips the fleece of a sheep.

- Australia produces many different kinds of fruits and vegetables. These include apples, oranges, potatoes, carrots, and tomatoes. Tropical fruits such as mangos and pineapples also grow there.
- Nickel is mined in southwestern Australia and used to make stainless steel and coins.

Tourism   Manufacturing   Oil   Fishing   Ranching

Mining   metal   opals   diamonds   sheep

Farming   sugarcane   dairy   fruit   wheat   cows

Arafura
Sea

Timor Sea

Indian Ocean

Coral Sea

AUSTRALIA

Tropic of Capricorn

Lightning
Ridge mine

Anna Creek
Station

Coober Pedy
mine

Pacific Ocean

Great
Australian Bight

N
W   E
S

NEW ZEALAND

South Island

Australia and New Zealand are known for
producing great wine. Southeastern Australia
and the northeastern part of New Zealand's
South Island grow the most wine grapes.

A New Zealand vineyard

25

Transportation

Transportation across the continent of Australia is difficult. The rough land of the Outback makes ground travel dangerous.

But despite that fact, a north-south railway system connects the cities of Darwin and Adelaide. There is also an east-west railway that connects Perth to Melbourne and Sydney.

Several good major highways connect Australia's major cities as well.

Australia's major seaports include Sydney, Melbourne, Brisbane, Newcastle, Hay Point, and Port Hedland. People and goods move to and from these ports.

Australia's rivers

Most of Australia's rivers are not used to transport goods. Because of the dry climate, areas of the rivers can become too shallow to sail on. As a result, river traffic is made up mostly of private boats.

The Ghan

The Ghan is a passenger train that has been used for more than 70 years. At first, the Ghan connected the cities of Alice Springs and Adelaide. In 2004, the railway was extended to Darwin.

A trip on the Ghan is a two-night journey and covers 1,847 miles (2,979 kilometers).

Moving around New Zealand

In New Zealand, State Highway 1 runs from Cape Reinga, at the tip of the North Island, to Stirling Point, on the southern end of the South Island. Ferryboats take cars and people across Cook Strait. In addition to roads and boats, trains are also used for transportation. Auckland and Wellington have trains that run to the suburbs and back into the cities.

- Australia's highways stretch for more than 496,000 miles (793,600 kilometers).
- Australia has about 450 airports. Most of them have paved runways.

Major Transportation Routes

— major highway — major railroad

● place of interest

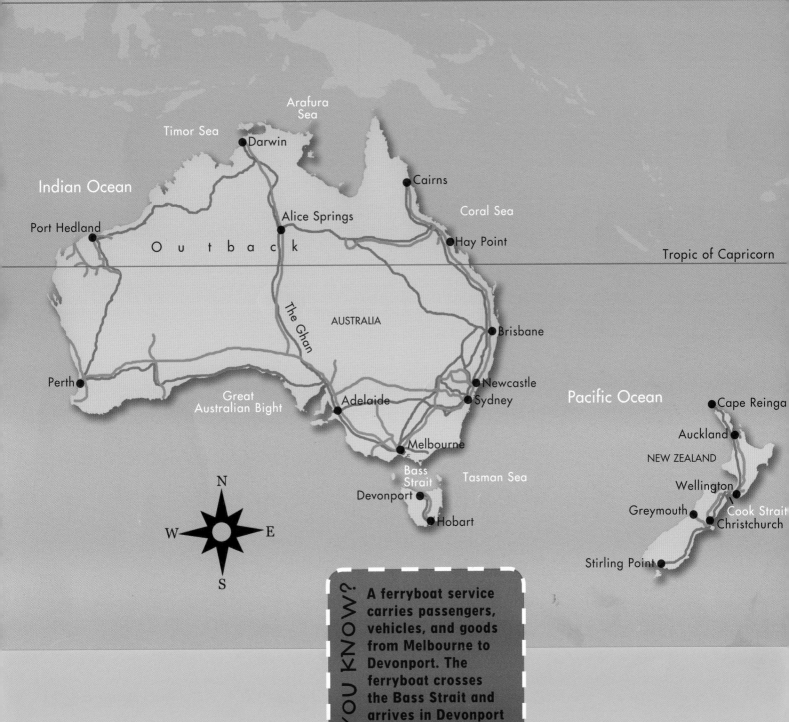

Equator

Arafura Sea

Timor Sea

Darwin

Indian Ocean

Cairns

Alice Springs

Coral Sea

Port Hedland

Outback

Hay Point

Tropic of Capricorn

The Ghan

AUSTRALIA

Brisbane

Perth

Great Australian Bight

Newcastle

Sydney

Pacific Ocean

Cape Reinga

Adelaide

Auckland

NEW ZEALAND

Melbourne

Bass Strait

Tasman Sea

Wellington

Devonport

Greymouth

Cook Strait

Christchurch

Hobart

Stirling Point

N
W   E
S

DID YOU KNOW? A ferryboat service carries passengers, vehicles, and goods from Melbourne to Devonport. The ferryboat crosses the Bass Strait and arrives in Devonport after a nine-hour trip.

Journey to the Great Barrier Reef

The blades of the helicopter whir as it rises from Gladstone, on the northeastern coast of Australia. It heads out to sea. It's carrying scientists on a visit to the Great Barrier Reef.

From the air, the edge of the reef is marked by a line of white surf. The line is where the waves of the Coral Sea break on the wall of coral.

The scientists are here to explore the underwater coral. The coral shines pink, yellow, bright blue, and orange. It looks like an underwater garden.

Wearing snorkels and masks, the scientists dive into the blue water. They explore the coral and the thousands of different sea creatures that make it their home.

Turning to avoid a mass of floating jellyfish, the scientists find what they are hunting for—a starfish feeding on the coral. Some starfish are the reef's most dangerous enemies. Scientists are still looking for ways to limit the damage they do to the coral reef.

Days later, the scientists visit Hook Reef, a part of the Great Barrier Reef. They hire a boat to take them to Dunk Island. Here they spot thousands of seabirds building their nests on the reef.

At last the boat arrives in Cairns, a bustling city on the coast. It is one of two main shipping channels (paths) through the reef. Elsewhere, only a few skilled fishermen and sailors can find a safe way through these shallow waters.

The jagged coral has grown, over hundreds of thousands of years, into a true "barrier."

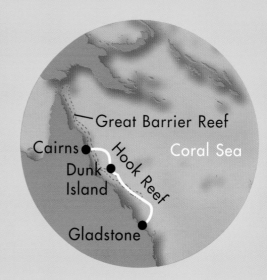

How coral reefs grow
Coral is formed in the sea by millions of tiny animals called polyps. When the polyps die, they leave behind their limestone skeletons. These skeletons form the barriers and ridges in the sea known as coral reefs.

29

Australia At-a-Glance

Continent size: the smallest of Earth's seven continents

Number of countries: one

Major languages:
- Aboriginal languages
- Chinese
- English
- Italian

Total population: 20.4 million (2007 estimate)

Most populated city: Sydney

Climate: dry most or all year with hot summers and warm to cold winters throughout most of the continent; tropical in the far north and northeast; mild in the far southwest, southeast, and eastern coast

Highest point: Mount Kosciuszko, 7,356 feet (2,229 meters)

Lowest point: Lake Eyre, 50 feet (15 m) below sea level

Longest river: Murray River

Largest body of water: Lake Eyre

Largest desert: Great Victoria Desert

Major agricultural products:
- barley
- cattle
- dairy products
- fruits
- poultry
- sheep
- sugarcane
- wheat

Major industries:
- agriculture
- fishing
- manufacturing (transportation equipment, chemicals, and steel)
- mining

Natural resources:
- bauxite
- coal
- copper
- diamonds
- gold
- iron ore
- lead
- mineral sands
- natural gas
- nickel
- petroleum
- silver
- tungsten
- uranium
- zinc

Glossary

Aborigines – the native people of Australia

barrier – material that blocks passage

basin – an enclosed or partly enclosed water area

bight – a bay formed by a bend in a coastline

body of water – a mass of water that is in one area; such as a river, lake, or ocean

climate – the average weather a place has from season to season, year to year

compass rose – a symbol used to show direction on a map

continent – one of seven large land masses on Earth, including Africa, Antarctica, Asia, Australia, Europe, North America, and South America

crops – plants that are grown in large amounts and are used for food or income

desert – a hot or cold, very dry area that has few plants growing on it

ecosystem – all of the living and nonliving things in a certain area, including plants, animals, soil, and weather

equator – an imaginary line around Earth; it divides the northern and southern hemispheres

exporter – one that sells goods to other countries

forest – land covered by trees and plants

formation – a single structure of rock

glacier – a large body of ice spreading down a slope or across a valley or land surface

grassland – land covered mostly with grass

highland – high or hilly land

island – land that is completely surrounded by water

lake – a body of water that is completely surrounded by land

landform – a natural feature on Earth's surface

legend – the part of a map that explains the meaning of the map's symbols

mountain – a mass of land that rises high above the land that surrounds it

natural resources – materials such as water, trees, and minerals that are found in nature

North Pole – the northern-most point on Earth

ocean – the large body of saltwater that covers most of Earth's surface

peninsula – a body of land that is surrounded by water on three sides

plateau – a large, flat, and often rocky area of land that is higher than the surrounding land

population – the total number of people who live in one area

port – a place where ships can load or unload cargo (goods or people)

rain forest – a thick forest that receives a lot of rain year-round

ranching – the work of raising animals such as cattle and sheep on a ranch

reef – a chain of coral on a bed of sand near the surface of the water

river – a large stream of water that empties into a lake, ocean, or other river

scale – the size of a map or model compared to the actual size of things they stand for

South Pole – the southern-most point on Earth

temperature – how hot or cold something is

wetland – an area that has very wet soil and is covered with water at least part of the year

Index

On the Web

FactHound offers a safe, fun way to find Web sites related to topics in this book. All of the sites on FactHound have been researched by our staff.

1. Visit www.facthound.com
2. Type in this special code: 1404838813
3. Click on the FETCH IT button.

Your trusty FactHound will fetch the best sites for you!

Look for all of the books in the Picture Window Books World Atlases series:

Atlas of Africa
Atlas of Australia
Atlas of Europe
Atlas of North America
Atlas of South America
Atlas of Southwest and Central Asia
Atlas of the Far East and Southeast Asia
Atlas of the Poles and Oceans